DAN FREEMAN

Dan Freeman

by Dan Jaffe

Illustrated by Aaron G. Pyle

UNIVERSITY OF NEBRASKA PRESS · LINCOLN

Publishers on the Plains

UNP

To

Rudolph and Elsie Umland

and

Fred and Fern Christensen

CONTENTS

Foreword   ix

I. A New Geography

Too Urgent to Deceive the World   3
North of the Paddock Hotel   4

II. The Filing

Winter on Summer   9
The Trade   11
Waltzing Toward Another Year   15

III. Breaking Ground

The Cannon Ball   19
On a Day of Slanting Rain   21
The Crossing   22
Dan Freeman Answers the Voice out of the Whirlwind   24
The Ledger   26
We Work with What's at Hand   28
A Tasty Day   30

IV. In Court

Number One   33
We Shall Not Abide Thee, Daniel Freeman   36
We Filed Our Teeth on Trouble   37
He'll Keep Right on Hooting   38

V. Hanging On

Night Talk   41
Journey to Montrose, 1903   44
Down in the Creek Bed   47

Freeman's the Name   50
Elegy   52
From the Top of the Knoll   53
They Buried Him on a Wind-Swept Afternoon   54

VI. The Legacy

The Purpose of Fragments   57
Levels   59

Dan Freeman Chronology   61
Appendix   63
A Note on Sources   72

FOREWORD

My grandfather, Max Jaffe, in his eighties sometimes still startles his children and grandchildren by clambering to the roof to putter around the chimney of his house in Elizabeth, New Jersey. Shortly after the turn of the century he crawled out of Russia, hiding in ditches as the Cossacks galloped by. After he discovered his America, he turned from cabinet making to carpentry to construction, made and lost a fortune, and each year grew more impassioned in his praise of God.

Grandpa gave us our name and our country, but it was a name out of the shadows, an Americanization of an uncertainty, a name that back beyond my grandfather's memory had been changed for reasons hidden in turbulent Russia. But it was the name he lived by, and so my birth certificate read Daniel Freeman Jaffe. A combination of three names: the first, sure as my grandfather's faith; the last, deceptive as history; the middle, a coincidental announcement of renewed independence, a compromise between Frohman and Friedman, between my father's enthusiasm for a man of the theater and his love for my mother's family.

Early in September, 1958, I rattled out of New Jersey in a five-year-old Chevrolet. I revved it up toward the Midwest, that nowhere most Easterners believe extends beyond the Appalachians. On balding tires, my motor pinging, I had set out to plumb a continent I only half-imagined. But in my head was New York, in my mouth, Newark. I expected to return much like an explorer back from the Poles. In the meantime I would speculate on the unusual and suffer the intolerable bravely.

Three days later I crossed the Missouri River into Nebraska City. For two hundred miles I'd felt sure I'd somersault suddenly into an Iowa ditch. Each time I'd felt the car tilt, the slanting curbstones of the narrow highway under my wheels, I expected to roll over. I was too tired to note the "quaint" any more. Things were as they were.

Somewhere between Nebraska City and Lincoln I noticed my gas gauge. It registered nearly empty. I drove mile after mile, hoping a station would appear around the next curve or over the next hill. At any moment I would sputter to a stop. I'd have to hitch a ride God knows how far and somehow get gas. But there were no cars coming or going. The sun, like a reddish-orange melon, rested in my way at the top of a hill up ahead. I stopped for a moment and looked for a farmhouse, a road sign. Nothing. I could look in four directions and see no signs of human habitation, no signs of man except for the roadside fences and the cement highway. Even a billboard would have given me solace at that moment. I was far from the stoops of New Jersey, far from the layers of metropolitan man, and I was unaccountably afraid.

I drove on into Lincoln feeling a new kinship for all men, especially for those who had looked squarely out across an unpeopled horizon, who had faced an uncharted landscape alone. I had come west to test the compass of myself and to weather a new geography.

Not until I had lived in Nebraska for more than a year and had come in many ways to feel more like a Midwesterner than an Easterner, despite my accent, did I learn about Daniel Freeman, the pioneer settler whose claim to be the first homesteader was recognized by the Congress. Finding I shared his name was like laying claim to history. Dan Freeman had settled not far from the geographical center of the continental United States. He had filed for his land on the same day the Emancipation Proclamation supposedly went into effect. He was a frontier iconoclast who felt bound to live up to his name, to exercise his freedom proudly, unpopular as he might become. I shared the name of a man who had consciously tried to make himself a myth but whose history is obscured by contradiction. At the center of the continent I'd found my namesake, and I meant to track him down.

Not long ago I received a letter from a lady editor of one of the most widely circulated American magazines, a magazine edited, of course, in the East. The lady commented about something I had written and expressed some curiosity about how I could stand it out on the dull, dusty plains. She could not have anticipated the temper of my reply. She had assumed that no one of good sense would ever willingly leave the environs of the great Eastern city, that I must be a captive of circumstances. Her letter disturbed me because it reminded me of my own early misconceptions.

Twelve years ago I would never have questioned or even cared to question an article in a leading news magazine referring to the "tundra" of western Kansas. I wouldn't have questioned because the Midwest was only an imaginary place, a television backdrop. This book is the result of my discovering the enormity of my delusion.

It is because the Midwest *is* that I have tried to capture who Dan Freeman *was*. I have tried to be as scrupulous as possible, to pin down facts as absolutely as I could. In both the poems and the prose I mean to make available to readers an actual man and the myth he created. I might have liked him different in some ways, but I did not purposely change him. That would have been like changing my name.

I do not know whether this is a literary or a historical work. That distinction is probably a false one. But this is not a report. Merely to learn about Freeman is not the same as to share his life and thereby a portion of his time and his land. I have tried to provide the reader with the latter opportunity.

Almost everything in this book could be footnoted, with certain obvious exceptions. Having said that, I choose to leave out the footnotes so that readers will read this as life rather than as a text. Nevertheless, some readers may want to know more about Dan Freeman's activities. Therefore, at the end of the book I've included a chronology and some notes.

If anything here does work for you, then share with me my appreciation for the help furnished by the staffs of the Homestead National Monument, the Nebraska Historical Society, and Dean F. Brandt, clerk of the Gage County District Court.

A grant from the Kansas City Institute of Trusts and Foundations through the University of Kansas City, now the University of Missouri at Kansas City, helped make my work easier. A number of unfortunate lines might have made their way into print if my wife, Yvonne, hadn't giggled so convincingly. Of course, no one who writes about Nebraska pioneer days can pay homage enough to the example and character of Mari Sandoz, who in the midst of her own work corresponded with me about this book.

I

A NEW GEOGRAPHY

I was born eight miles from a railroad, five miles from a schoolhouse, nine miles from a church, 885 miles from New York, 220 yards from a swimming hole, and 15 feet from a cornfield.

Statement of R. H. Harris, *a Lynch, Nebraska, pioneer on a visit to the Homestead National Monument*

Too urgent to deceive the world,
To pocket more than bits of fact
And parts of poems, I tracked the years
Down school-boy corridors to streets
Of promised payoff in the dark,
Through sleepless traffic wheeling westward,
Finding myself, at last, alone,
Unsettled by a prairie night.

Baffled by silent distances,
Bent by the heaviness of sky,
I braced beneath the crush of stars,
Forced to the bedrock of myself.
As if made literal by need,
All the ambiguous years returned
To give my presence substance, buttress
My stance against the push of time.

NORTH OF THE PADDOCK HOTEL

In the Paddock Hotel, at the edge of Freeman's Corner,
A farm equipment salesman from Colorado
Told me directions, but not until he bragged
He knew every back road, every short-cut
Through Nebraska. He reckoned he knew the state
Better than folks who'd lived there all their lives.
Been selling the country for years and the people,
"Good folks, the salt of the earth." But he missed the mountains.
In the lobby behind him the pensioners rocked,
Gazing out windows at the weather,
Remembering, at moments, sudden storms or heat waves
Back when they was pups and hunted rabbits
With the Freeman boys or the mad old man himself.

Nobody outlives Nebraskans except Tibetans
They say. Chamber of Commerce spokesmen claim,
"Folks here live long enough to pay their debts."
They outlive allergies. Patches of tossing
Goldenrod, the state flower, startle
The pale, soot-lunged Easterners passing through.

I trudged north, four scorching blocks, to the courthouse,
A porched brick rectangle rebuilt too late
To save the records of the town's first years.
Outside on the walk, between rows of elms,
I stod before the War Memorial,
A sandstone pyramid, its top sliced off,
The names of heroes and ordinary men
Indistinguishable, a fading tally
Of volunteers in almost forgotten wars.
Finally I found his name, *Daniel Freeman*
Of the *Seventeenth Illinois Infantry*.
So monuments make history of rumors.

[4]

The name in the crumbling stone was my name, too.
But what real part of me except as dreams
That reoccur are real? How did Dan'l,
Cussing his neighbors, "Bible-reading fools,"
Sluicing tobacco juice from off his porch,
Change me, the orthodox Jersey Jew whose name,
By chance alone, was his? What Babylonian
Magic had charmed me 'cross a continent
To find myself, then hid our secret bond
Behind the years, beyond deciphering?
Daniel Freeman, whatever man you were
I share now, as I share the myths you made
With all our countrymen. And you as far
From me as the tamer of lions who named us both!
But we are linked fast as the cannon balls
Welded to the base of this monument.
I stoop and finger them, Gettysburg
And the wars we have survived, wondering how
After boys rolled them down Beatrice* streets
To thunder in Midwestern Halloweens
The town historian recovered them.
How did he snatch back history from ghosts
And fetch it here to decorate our lives?

*Pronounced Be-at' -rice.

II

THE FILING

... to Gage County belongs the honor of having secured the first live homesteader under the U. S. Homestead Law. . . . Dan Freeman still lives and flourishes on his original homestead. . . . Mr. Freeman says he has seen a great many things in his time . . . and will not pay us a cent for this notice and picture of his place.

Beatrice Express, December 28, 1876

WINTER ON SUMMER

Winter on summer, hail
On heat, grit
On stone. Between
Horizons, between plains
And sky, against each other
And against ourselves.
What presses us,
Dan Freeman, toward manhood
And toward madness?
This season is war, as always,
And so: begin.

Before dawn one morning in late June, 1862, Dan Freeman saddled up. He hadn't much time; he wanted to buy the rights to a claim as quickly as possible. Harris, the squatter on the claim he had his eye on, might sell. Word in Beatrice had it that Harris's missus was restless, that Harris might be induced to leave the land. But Harris needed a means of conveyance. Dan Freeman meant to supply it.

Freeman rode out the old Indian trail—freighters called it the St. Deroin Trail—that connected with the Oregon Trail at Fort Kearny. Just off the trail, near Cub Creek, four miles west of Beatrice, Harris had built a log cabin under three big oaks. He had done little else besides break some sod and plant some corn and flax. Dense brush hugged three sides of the cabin, and weeds sprouted from its sod roof. But Freeman didn't care. He could imagine himself planted there and thriving.

But first he had to settle with Harris, who, under the Pre-emption Act of 1841, held first rights to purchase the land or file on it when the new Homestead Act went into effect on the first of the year. Harris probably hadn't entered the claim as a pre-emption, but Freeman wanted it legal. There was little claim-jumping in Gage County, and folks knew where Harris had settled.

The claim was worth trading for. Cub Creek would supply water and timber. There was a cabin ready to move into. He wouldn't be far from Beatrice, which looked like it might become a lively town. And there would always be folks coming along the trail, folks he could chat with or barter with when they watered their horses. If Harris wanted to move anyway, thought Free-man, maybe he'd settle for a team of oxen.

THE TRADE

I

Through clockless days,
Pulled by the high hands of the sun,
He plodded in the shadow of his mule.

Two leather arcs,
Heavy as the voiceless miles,
Drooped from the haunches, knotted into fists,

Twin traces
Echoing the curving land.
Across the bow-bend of the afternoon

Lines of geese,
Flushed from Dakota by the scent
Of snow, arrowed south, chilling the air.

The squatter swore;
The mule's tail swatted wind;
The moldboard wrenched against the hardening land.

II

Spring gnawed at the snow,
Stirred within his cabin walls,
Upturned the secret bones buried in sod.

Beside Cub Creek
The mule's skull stared at the blinking sun,
A slow contemplation of the quickening days

Bleaching toward summer.
By April, as the prairie pulsed, sudden
Strings of buffalo shouldered the westward sky,

[11]

Snorting rain,
While tumbleweeds somersaulted east,
Like hoopsnakes, chasing the stampeding clouds

Back all the way,
To St. Looey's fashions, to rigs and cobbles,
To the froth of paddlewheelers New Orleans bound.

III

But the days clogged.
No easy trails swept back through time,
Back past Sumter and rebellion's weather.

The stiffening mud
Of spring sucked at his soddy's walls,
Clutched at his feet as if the ground had hands.

Even the rivers
Rattled chains below the tide,
Tugged at rusting links gripping their banks.

Only a rare ghost,
A Pawnee brave on a lean pony,
Brief as far-off lightning on summer nights,

Drifted trackless
And free in the twilight over the rise.
Further back in the dark a coyote complained to the moon.

IV

Soon after dawn
A black-coated rider reined up,
A tall, bearded stranger, stained from the trail.

[12]

Rider and squatter
Measured speech, kicked at the dirt.
As the horse nosed the creek they talked of war and weather.

No longer a stranger
Dan Freeman galloped east. The squatter,
Who'd agreed to trade his claim, walked the land

No longer his.
Was it those eyes, insistent as flames?
Or Freeman's wind-singed beard? Or the promised oxen

Muscled as the land
He'd traded? Or Freeman's words: "A man
With such a team could budge the continent!"?

At the stroke of the new year, Dan Freeman stepped up to file for the first homestead certificate issued at the Brownville, Nebraska, land office. Years afterward, when he told how he happened to become the first homesteader, he always began by explaining how he happened to be in Brownville and why he had to file at midnight. Sometimes he said that as a young soldier he had been assigned to the secret service and stationed there, sometimes that he had been detailed to Brownville on special assignment, sometimes that he was on furlough. He told his daughter, Eliza, that he had been stationed nearby on the Little Blue River to keep watch on the Indians; his son Sam, on the other hand, believed that he was a Pinkerton. But no matter how Dan Freeman told his story, he always said he had to be on the trail early on New Year's Day, 1863. As soldier, secret service agent, or Pinkerton, he had to report to St. Louis or elsewhere. He had been reassigned or was "due to take his place again in the ranks on the tented fields." If he didn't file as soon as the Homestead Act went into effect, he might not be able to secure his land at all.

And so when he encountered the clerk of the Brownville land office at a New Year's Eve ball for prospective settlers, Freeman immediately said "it would be a great accommodation" if the clerk would allow him to file his application at once. After he had told his story, Freeman's spark struck kindling. In a territory where 10 per cent of the population had volunteered for service in the Union cause, his story was bound to find sympathetic, unquestioning ears.

Arrangements were made, the land office opened, and Freeman's filing completed shortly after the New Year began.

WALTZING TOWARD ANOTHER YEAR!

Waltzing toward another year
To fiddles and a banjo,
The Brownville belles dipped and sighed
As the old year drifted out and died.

They wheeled around the hotel floor
To the thump of frontier boots,
And the river clock kept time outside
As the old year settled in the tide.

While they waltzed toward 1863,
Another year of war,
Dan Freeman read some papers through
Explaining what he'd have to do.

"I'm ready to sign, just tell me where,"
He told the registrar.
The lamp jets danced; clocks said "New Year!"
The land office clerk, "Mr. Freeman, sign here."

III

BREAKING GROUND

When they cut sod with the old rod
plows, the roots of the prairie grasses
sang a tune.

Dale Sherman Whitcomb, *a native
of Beatrice who knew Freeman*

For some reason, after he had filed on the 160 acres of Section 26 in Township 4 (Blakely) of Range 5, the parcel of land that was to become known as Homestead No. 1, Dan Freeman, despite his supposed duties as a soldier or Pinkerton, drifted back home to Knox County, Illinois. There he learned that his younger brother James was missing, perhaps dead. James, who was engaged to Agnes Suiter, a pretty Le Claire girl he'd met at Abingdon College.

Freeman set out to find his brother. Rumor had it that the 83rd Illinois Infantry was at Gettysburg, so he headed there. But he did not find James among the maimed men and riddled fields. Instead he carried away an eight-pound cannon ball, a hard memory of a brother. More than a year later he learned that James had died of exposure and sickness at Fort Donelson. Each day death became more personal. In 1861, just after the war started, Dan Freeman's wife, Elizabeth, had died in Rock Island. Agnes must feel as he did then.

THE CANNON BALL

Flash floods at dawn, rivers red with clay;
By noon a cracking sun, wind rasping my bones.
Behind me Gettysburg, the black muskets
Splintered, Brother James stiffened by rumor,
His only grave in my unsodded mind.
I carry death inside my saddlebags;
Its heaviness thumps the flanks of my sweating bay;
I feel its iron roughness in my bones.
We rode together, Brother, stalwart as muskets,
Ready as boys tracking a lusty rumor
Through the tall grass. Oh, what fool's gold we mined,
Wrapped in the glitter of spring! Our bravest flags
Rot now in the fields of Gettysburg where muskets
Rust beside the helter-skelter bones
Wrenched from their springs, and I hear a bodiless rumor
Walking the groves, whimpering like the wind.
My legs are stiff in the stirrups as twin muskets,
For I carry you in the litter of my bones,
James, the cannon ball pressing my side like a tumor.
But I will plant it soon, at sundown salute it with muskets,
A new grave in a land without old stones.
And if a dark truth grows, these hands will husk it.

Dan Freeman returned to Beatrice in the summer of 1864. In August, with a band of citizens, he galloped to head off the marauding Cheyennes before they reached Gage County. They engaged the hostiles briefly in Nuckolls County, then rode back to Beatrice where nervous townspeople had thrown up sod breastworks. But the excitement didn't last long, and Daniel soon felt lonely.

And so he married James's Agnes, in Scott County, Iowa, on February 8, 1865. He was her second choice, and she, his. For a short while they visited relatives in Iowa and Illinois. Then in a dirty combination car, at a speed of fifteen miles an hour, they bounced west to Nebraska City. There in a downpour Daniel hitched up a team of black ponies to a light wagon for the trip to the homestead.

The Blue was running bank full when they reached Beatrice. Daniel sent Agnes and her oak hope chest across on a flat boat. With two men helping, he floated the wagon across on a pile of driftwood. Sure she would soon be a widow, Agnes waited on the opposite bank.

ON A DAY OF SLANTING RAIN

No time for crossing:
A horizontal day of slanting rain,
The Big Blue rumpled as wind-loosened canvas,
Agnes, drenched pale in the wagon,
Uncomplaining.
                    I think of willows,
Of white birches, leaning through gusts,
Through wars, the skirmishers
Snapping branches in their rush.

The rain
On Brother James, somewhere still,
Like Agnes's gentle tears, seeps down
And waters my stubborn love.
It washes us west, washes out
Those easy glories we imagined.
But the land will grow us more.

THE CROSSING

Kept company by thunder, we rumbled westward
Through an almost storyless land punctuated by rain,
Through twilight to an unnamed river that poured
Suddenly, like night, across the plain.

The horses balked, then slowly started forward,
Hooves light on the deck, as if the earth were slipping.
The Conestoga wagon creaked aboard,
Wheels heavy with mud, streaked canvas dripping.

A swarthy boatman unhitched the fraying line;
We sung out, into the mist, broadside,
Into a long rush, darker than the Rhine,
Of shadows spilling seaward with the tide.

We hung from the guide rope, motionless in midstream,
Feeling the wet strands tighten, the raft sway,
A current shudder through the white-eyed team.
The river tugged from under, down and away.

From the rear of the raft the boatman hollered, "Friend,
Before you reached this crossing, what was your name?
I list all the sad souls that the fates send."
I shouted back at him through the rain, "The same

As it is! Same as it's likely to remain."
He came out of the mist, knife in hand,
In a cavernous voice repeated, "Your name? Your name?"
Ready to slash at the line that joined us to land.

I saw, as if in moonlight, the blade shine,
Ready to cut us loose for torrents to toss
Like driftwood; and I leaped on him just in time,
"Dan Freeman's the name, and I intend to cross!"

When Dan and Agnes reached the homestead, they found Nathan Blakely waiting with the small Charter Oak stove he'd borrowed before Daniel left. Agnes would use that stove until the doors burned out around the edges and ashes from the firebox sifted down on the baking bread. She had come west to settle the claim on Cub Creek, to firm it up with family, to chop the heads off chickens on a stump in the yard, to churn, to bear Eliza in the squatter's hut, then, before it fell to ruin, surrender it to the horses.

With timber from the creek bed, Freeman built another cabin. He chinked the walls with mud, slabbed the roof with sod, dug a shallow draw to the creek. He and Agnes tramped in and out on free soil, hoarded rain in a barrel, and dug coops for the chickens in the knoll out back.

Buffalo were rare, but he scavanged along the Republican and the Big Sandy, then sold what he wouldn't touch himself. When he was gone, Agnes kept the window covered to keep Indians from peering in at her. They scared her almost sick. J. W. Burns maintained that he'd been ambushed along the creek not far away by one of the varmints named Black Bob. And Old Man Whitcomb said that once, before Freeman's time, injuns had tied a white man to a tree and scalped him; Whitcomb pointed out the notch. Daniel wasn't fazed. He just showed off two scars he said came from Sioux bullets. Anyway, the Otos were friendly, not given to scalpings.

But Agnes fretted, periodically threatened to go back to Illinois for good, worried over Liza and their three boys, Sam, Jim, and John. And year after year she bore the spectacle of Daniel beating the devil around a stump yet staying within the law.

DAN FREEMAN ANSWERS THE VOICE OUT OF THE WHIRLWIND

On this bulge of the plain I rode from Ohio
    and Illinois, out of the sun that rocked
    me through Iowa and blinked me here,

On this rib of the tilting continent where
    my heels caught on a clod of an aspened
    hill beside Cub Creek, strung like a
    beaded promise through an almost desert
    bound yet to bloom,

I shall weather the open mouth of the tornadoing
    air, the spill of snow pressing the lids
    of life, nine circles of prairie fire,
    and the impassivity of the crusted land.

If you walk about a quarter of a mile east of the Freeman home-stead, out into the pasture about a hundred yards north of the highway, you can see the wagon ruts of the old St. Deroin Trail. Freighters and homesteaders traveling along that trail often stopped at the Freeman place. Dan Freeman invariably would march out to welcome them, offer them Cub Creek's clear water and any loose timber. He asked only that they not destroy the trees or kill the birds. Dan liked to talk to passers-by, to figure out that he and they were somehow distantly related or knew the same folks back east. And he liked to tell them his story, about how he filed and became Number One.

Freeman's visitors were men like John Edward Bryant, who left Martinsville, Indiana, early in April, 1873, to homestead in Nebraska with his young wife. They remembered proudly having shared yellow biscuits with the man who secured the first land under the homestead law. And he remembered them. He kept a guest book that hundreds of travelers signed.

THE LEDGER

They always scratched their letters out like claims
Across the bareness of his ledger's pages,
Left trails of ink he blotted into names.
He waved them westward. In wagons and in stages
They scrawled across the land and wrote their days
Into the sod. Svendson and Axelweight,
Wheeler and Cole, dimmed in horizon's haze
As Dan'l scanned his book and penned each date.

Flintlock and powder horn hung from his wall:
Revolutionary relics, holy as that war,
Grandfather Freeman's markers for them all.

One Independence Day he posed in the door
One hand 'round the barrel of the long squirrel gun,
The kind Boone carried, another name that mattered.
A small crowd cheered for "Homestead No. 1."
When he fired west, everybody scattered!
Then he made speech, explained it hadn't been
Part of a plan he'd meant to carry out,
But because of his name, because he was a Freeman
Things naturally just had to come about,
That he was named for Boone, and that helped, too.
He asked each man kindly to sign his name.
Some laughed, but the columns slowly grew,
Rippling in the sun and into fame.

Up and down Cub Creek they all agreed, even Daniel Freeman, who liked to stand, back against a tree, foot on a stump, and tell them all they didn't know a prairie chicken. They needed a school! Not a soul denied it. In the Freeman's second cabin, Agnes had taught the first class in the district, seven neighbor boys, for total pay of twenty-one dollars a term year.

After the district's log school burned down back in October, 1873, Agnes began poking Daniel to build another. One that wouldn't turn to tinder the first prairie fire that came along. One that was close enough so that the children wouldn't cry from the cold on their way to and from it in the middle of winter. She reminded him he owed her, from the first term she'd taught. She reminded him he'd taken her teaching money, all twenty-one dollars, to buy an axe and other doodads. Daniel waited and measured sentiment up and down the creek before he started what he knew he'd have to finish.

Tom Freeman, whom Daniel called "Cousin" though there wasn't any blood between them, had dug a kiln into the terrace on the west side of the creek just north of the road. He'd been operating it for two years. And though Tom was a South Carolinian and Daniel was a Yankee, proud of his Vermont heritage, Tom taught him how to make bricks from the native soil. So in 1875 they built a school together, just a quarter mile west of the Freeman cabin.

We work with what's at hand.
What if sweat drips from our beards!
We'll make a firmness
That won't crumble if you knead it hard.
Tom says, "These bricks'll last a hundred years,"
Enough to be remembered by.
Agnes says, "Dan Freeman, build
That school and even I'll be proud."
So I'll do it,
For now and later.
Each brick is like a quarter section
You can wrap a paw around.
And you can lay them up
And call it Freeman School.

Dan Freeman liked to say that Nebraska was the finest state in the Union; Gage, the finest county in the state; and his homestead, the finest in the county. When he and Agnes settled, you could still practically live off the land. Mink, skunk, and raccoon were plentiful. There were wild plums to gather. There were prairie chickens in flocks as big as a henyard, and antelope and deer so tame they'd mix in with the cattle.

Dan prided himself on being an agriculturist, a tree-planter, a protector of wild life. From the start he experimented. In 1873 he put in about 35 acres of corn, 30 acres of wheat, rye, and oats, 10 acres of potatoes, 20 acres of white beans, five acres of tobacco, and an acre of onions. He meant to be a scientific farmer, and they said diversification was "a remedy to many ills of the soil." He was proud of his successes and every now and then stopped in at the local newspaper office to exhibit his produce—as in July of 1876, when he delivered several stalks of white winter wheat that had "headed very full." "Dan thinks," said the Express, "that the piece from which it was taken will yield at least 25 bushels to the acre." He even sent a sample to the Centennial Exposition in Philadelphia.

Dan fancied himself as a horse breeder, too. At one time he owned seventy-five horses. You could usually find him by locating his team of spotted ponies.

After twenty years on the homestead, he was still trying the new. In October, 1876, he stocked a pond on his place with German carp from the fishery commission at South Bend.

He had always planted trees. He set out elms and walnuts around the brick house built in 1876, and a grove of cottonwood and Osage orange trees to shade the approach. After a rain he would walk in his apple and cherry orchard, glad to feel the shaken drops, walking unconcernedly through water standing in depressions down the rows. He meant to protect that fruit from the ravages of birds, but he believed he could do it without a gun.

A TASTY DAY

To save his apple and his cherry trees,
Dan Freeman planted mulberries,
An orchard full of briberies.

Who ever heard a blackbird sing?
Just gossiping and chattering
From morning until evening!

Till Dan'l feared that in his trees,
Bloodying their beaks on mulberries,
Like townsfolk arrogant as fleas,

They jeered at him, seeming to say:
"Cherries and apples across the way,
A tasty day! A tasty day!"

IV

IN COURT

Dan Freeman has gone into the practice of
law . . . . The other day he shone brilliantly
on the defense. Go in, Dan.

Beatrice Express, May 8, 1873

Dan Freeman could back a man into a corner with a stream of rhetoric, then smile from back of his beard as if it had all been a joke. Men thought he was bigger than he was, so he held public office—Gage County coroner, bailiff of the district court, sheriff. He also served as Justice of the Peace of Blakely District (his enemies called him "Injustice of the Peace") and as county commissioner.

But Dan struck his legal poses more often before the bench than behind it. For years litigation in which he was involved remained on the docket. He was such a courtroom regular that on January 15, 1887, the Express *saw fit to announce, "Dr. Dan Freeman, the man who filed the first homestead claim made in the United States, was rejoicing this week over the fact that the district court docket for the term did not contain his name as plaintiff or defendant, a thing which has not occurred before for a period of fifteen years." Not even John Suiter, Agnes' brother, who had filed for the homestead next to Freeman's, was exempt from a Freeman suit. In 1871, W. H. Ashby, a Beatrice lawyer ostensibly representing Agnes, managed to have the Suiter land attached, and in 1872 it was added to the Freeman spread.*

Even his children came to call him
By the name of myth, not *Father, Dad,*
But by the label that he gave himself,
Demanded of the world. And the town,
Of course, gloried in this whim,
If not in others. His claim was theirs
So long as no trouble was attached.
"Dan Freeman, the First Homesteader,
Lives just four miles west of here,"
The *Express* reported when it had the chance.

But they lived by the tales they were given to,
And by new ones plucked at random
Like columbine from the roadsides.
So Dan'l, who'd cultivated, harrowed,
Grew more than he had bargained for.

The magnification of the public eye
Turned motes to mysteries, Dan'l
To a sorcerer in doctor's gown
Who practiced secretly by night
On private illnesses too shameful
To be known. To all things desperate
He became their key; for his dark eyes,
They thought, fathomed the ways of stealth,
Of empty corrals, of scalpings, of the law.

Some dreamed him cutting circles in
The sod, malevolent as Faustus,
A dealer in bones and shadows who fetched
Up sin like 'hoppers from the Rockies.
Back with Agnes from Illinois,
He hallooed the ladies from behind his beard,
Half-bowed to the proper gingham, then stalked

Like Jehovah down Beatrice streets.
But neither his prophecies, his visions
Of tracks extending from his arms
Westward like two level pointers,
Nor his rumbled rhetoric,
Hushed rumors of his absences.
Tales of his atheist journeys
Filled their bawdiest imaginings
With wagons full of harem girls
Eager to stretch supine upon
The prairies, and Dan'l minister
To all the lusts they damned him for.

But he was their talisman, NUMBER ONE,
His claim authentic and recognized.
His was a gift out of which to grow.
And he, in spite of all, was theirs,
And justified them to themselves.

In his seventy-third year, Dan Freeman once again captured pub-
lic attention. He asked the district court of Gage County to forbid
the teaching of religion in the public schools. Nothing he did in
his life created greater controversy. He became the butt of jokes,
the notorious ally of Satan.

At the time, Freeman intended to enroll his nine-year-old
daughter, May Agnes, in the Freeman School, then attended by
his thirteen-year-old son, Le Clair. But first he sued the "Board
of School District No. 21 in the County of Gage and the State of
Nebraska" for allowing Miss Agnes Beecher, the daughter of a
local minister, to turn the school into a "place of public worship."
Freeman complained that during school hours Miss Beecher
regularly read portions of the King James version of the Bible to
the pupils, that she and the pupils sang from Gospel Hymns,
and that she offered up prayers in school according to the custom
of "what is known as the orthodox evangelical churches." He ob-
jected to paying taxes for the support of religion and to a par-
ticular religion being shown preference. Most startling, he stated
unequivocally that he did not believe in the "efficiency of prayers
. . . or the songs" and had "conscientious objections to the read-
ing from . . . the Bible."

When the school board refused to act, Dan began a long court
action that would not end until January, 1903. On October 9,
1902, the Nebraska Supreme Court decided that Miss Beecher had
violated the Nebraska Constitution; but the controversy refused
to subside, and the following year the Chief Justice issued a
ruling that the Bible could be read in school as literature.

Dan Freeman had won a shattering victory over the school
board. But at the same time he became the state's leading heathen,
the chief threat to the foundations of faith. The press, however,
took special pains to suggest that although Dan might have been
unreasonable, even perverse, in pressing his case, the Constitution
guaranteed the right of every man to be unreasonable in religious
matters.

WE SHALL NOT ABIDE THEE, DANIEL FREEMAN

The God-fearing men who prosper in this land
Sowed bountiful prayers, and the Good Lord richly answered.
Tassels sprout from green hymns, not from the sand
Of heresy. Let us praise the Bright Bird
Jesus, harken not to the scavenger crow
Who would revile us for our holiness,
Undo our father's deeds. The faith we know
Prospers our lives, blesses us as we bless.

Shall we, the children of the Lord, speak not
Of the Lord unto our children? Oh, Satan,
Though the tip of thy beard flame, still we shall not
Abide thee, by any name, Daniel Freeman
Or Mephistopheles. Ring the school bell!
Our hymns shall drive the devil back to hell.

WE FILED OUR TEETH ON TROUBLE

An injun hatchet nearly split my hide
The spring Cub Creek muddied our cabin wall.
My Agnes coughed so hard she almost died.
Hell, we limped through summer, then fall
Lightnin' set the prairie running wild
Before a man could get a bucket out.
Well, we're still here and cussin'. We filed
Our teeth on trouble. We know what it's about.
Right out back we fired bricks for a school,
Me and Tom. I guess we would again.
But now some goddamn politicking fool
Says Dan Freeman ain't American.
Did we chew locusts, drink dust from a sieve,
So a preacher's daughter could teach us how to live?

HE'LL KEEP RIGHT ON HOOTING

No, it's not the first time Dan'l's whacked
The biddies' backsides, then hooted for all to hear.
But Bible scoffing's different! Some who backed
Him once will find this shakes them by the scruff
When they run for public office. Old Number One's
Caught them in a mantrap set for thieves.
And he'll keep right on hooting till he's done,
While they try to pluck their chestnuts from the fire.
Dan'l won't renege. That's clear enough.
He's always been as manageable as sin.
He won't be handled like somebody's tool.
He won't be gaveled down. He's never been.
But like I've always said, even a fool
Has got a right to believe what he believes.

V

HANGING ON

Hé, my children, here is another pipe.
Now I am going to holler on this earth.
Everything is in motion.

Arapaho Ghost Dance Song

[39]

Dan Freeman bought, sold, claimed, sued for, acquired. By 1882 his 160 acres had grown to more than a thousand. Much of it he rented. But he cared about his tenants' success. He boasted that all his renters did so well they eventually bought farms of their own.

Everything grew, including the family. Dan and Agnes had eight children. As the children grew up, more and more buildings went up. And for one reason or another most of them went up in smoke. First, the boys burned down a shed. Then the two frame houses the boys moved into flamed into oblivion. Some thought the Freeman boys were pyromaniacs, but nobody ever dared suggest it to Daniel.

After Tom Freeman had taught him to make bricks from the soil, Dan constructed his own kiln. In 1876 he and Agnes finished building a big brick house. They built it for the future, intending to add on to it some day; but they never did. Eight years after Daniel's death, his and Agnes' old bedstead fell through flames from the second story.

NIGHT TALK

I've heard their young'uns,
"Look out! Don't step in the devil's shadow.
If he breathes on you, you'll
Plummet straight to hell."
I shake my beard at them,
And how they scamper.
Like rabbits from an owl.

But what they fear most, I believe.
Out in the dark, everyone asleep,
I've heard flint strike flint
And no one there to strike it.
I've listened to *Him*, behind the kiln,
Ordering his minions.
Till I finally understood
It was more than a critter
In the creek bed or an elm branch
Wrestling with the wind.

In '64 *He* set the plains ablaze,
Stampeding settlers east.
Some blamed King Fisher, a half-breed lunatic.
Just another name for *Him!*
He sets the world alight, and houses
Burn like kindling. Three times
He's dropped his line for us,
Hooked with flame.
It's like rubbing a burn
To think on my own name,
My youngest, Dan'l, Jr.,
A stone across the road.

They call me mad.
They say a madman's kin to the prince of darkness.

[41]

But who in this land hasn't tasted cinders?
Who hasn't had the devil in his mouth
And tried to spit him out?
Try spitting out your tongue.
Try dousing prairie fires with spit.

I tell myself, Dan Freeman,
You've walked on ashes.
But I never scuttled to the river
Or expected it to part.
I built again, of brick,
Of my own land, with my own hands.
And I would again.

In 1886, Dan Freeman felt prosperous. And so he sent a cane from his homestead to Galusha Grow, "Father of the Homestead Act"—Grow, who from the time of his first speech until, as Speaker of the House, he signed the Homestead Act, in season and out of season kept the policy of "free homes for free men" constantly before the Congress. Along with the cane Dan sent a letter in which he said:

> *My application for said patent was No. 1, my proof of residence No. 1, and the patent is recorded on Page 1, Volume 1, of the records at Washington. Hence this cane sent you was grown upon the land first taken under the said Homestead Act.*
>
> *Knowing well that the zealous and able efforts put forth by you to secure the passage of said act justly entitle you to be considered its father; and realizing that the said act is the greatest that has ever been passed by Congress, I feel that I, as one of its beneficiaries, am not overstepping the rules of propriety in presenting you with this simple token of my gratitude and appreciation.*

In 1903, Grow retired. The people of Montrose, Pennsylvania, his home town, welcomed home their most famous son. They felt it appropriate to invite for the occasion Daniel Freeman, the first settler under the act for which Grow had fought so hard. Dan'l, though now seventy-seven, consented at once. He greeted Grow at the railroad station and spoke from the same platform as the famous congressman.

"Agnes, let me be," he said.
"I'm goin'. I'd travel to hell itself
To meet Galusha Grow. Why,
Pennsylvania ain't more than a good ride
For a Freeman."

"Old man," said I,
"You'll take the train
Or I'll tie you down."

He smacked me on the rump
Like one of his spotted ponies.
"It's settled then," he said.
I should have known old Number One
Would have his way.

"You'll take the train
And a new suit as well. I won't
Have you mix with civilized folks
Looking like a squatter."

"Civilized folks be damned!"
Said he, tugging his beard.
"The West makes men. Galusha Grow
Can tell if there's a mule
Underneath a stovepipe."

"Dan Freeman, if you go east
You'll buy a suit," I said.
"You'll not embarrass me.
I've said it twice.
And that's that."

And then, imagine it,
He dropped his cane and bowed,
"Agnes, you're still a lady,
But you're tougher than the sod."

And so he shook Grow's hand,
Reviewed a parade from the courthouse steps,
At the fairgrounds
Even made a speech
In which he married me too late
And in the wrong state,
But remembered, of course,
That he was Number One.

Folks cheered for Galusha Grow
And for Dan Freeman, too!
And old Number One, he gloried
In those celebration pictures
Of him in his travel-creased clothes.
(He never did unpack the suit)
But I'm still mortified.

Old Number One wasn't feeling sprightly. But even though he was past eighty, he'd be damned before he'd miss hearing William Jennings Bryan. It was September, 1907, and Bryan had come to speak in Beatrice. In his "Victories of Peace" address he said: "The homestead was instrumental in bringing about a peaceful conquest of the desert west. It offered an inducement, a reward for the settlement and the result is that the desert has been made to blossom as a rose. The pioneers endured hardships and made their homes on the lonely prairie. They were men and women who gave the world more than they took from it.

"The first one to take advantage of the homestead act was a Freeman, and the name is a good one, for the law was framed to make free men and free people."

In the midst of Bryan's address, a voice from the crowd shouted, "He's here!" Up hobbled Dan Freeman. Bryan shook hands with the bearded old man, and Number One waved his cane at the crowd.

DOWN IN THE CREEK BED

Now that he's done changing much of anything
And nobody round about's impressed much by his myth,
You'd think that he'd let be. But no. His badgering
Won't stop. He slaps the barn door with his heavy palm
And spills a sluice of language that would make a preacher spit.

Even out of sight he's pestiferous as weeds,
Choking the air with banter, gab, and hollering
Till you wonder who it is down there he's jawing with.
You hear a heehaw or a guffaw or a galdarn
Sumpin' more than you'd like to, seeing that he's your kin.

    Dan'l, it aint so.
                  Doc, you mule's ass,
Who's Number One?
                       Them bastards named me sheriff once,
Then clean forgot. Damnation! Let 'em char in hell.
I can remember Gettysburg.
                         Trumpets, now!
Here's a vet can kiss the devil's butt and whistle
Dixie.
               I'll be around the day they bury you.

Like bonfire smoke their voices curl from the creek bed,
Rough enough, you'd think, to peel bark or strip sod.
I'll stop their mouthing before they scare the injun dead
Back to the war path from the burial ground, before
They dry us out by buttoning up the clouds or stunt
The corn by dirtying the air. It's devil's doin'.
Something sure has got old Dan'l by the soul.

And I swear I'll chase his friend right off, back to town,
To find some other folks less likely to be itched.
I clamber down the bank to shut their rising voices,
But they jumble into one, jumble into Dan'l's,
The names all his, *Sheriff*, and *Doc*, and *Number One*,
Dan'l through the years, with a flourish of his hat,
A snap of his suspenders, a half bow, a straight
Walk, a wave and spit over his shoulder, Dan'l
Meeting Dan'l, arguing and cussing with
Himself. And looking every part of him he played.

My insides hurt, I'll tell you, seeing him this way,
Living it through again, as if it ever was
Really like he told it to the world. But, Dan'l,
You always looked the part, and, Jesus, don't you still!
Cuss and spit. I'll cheer you, *Number One*. Go on
Believing. 'Cause if you can, by God, then we can, too.

In 1907, the Parker Company out of Atchinson, Kansas, thumped and skyrocketed its carnival into Beatrice to celebrate the fiftieth anniversary of the county. They set up just east of the fire station at Fifth and Market. The boys who checked tickets felt supremely honored, kings of the midway, vastly superior to the bearded old man who made a spectacle of himself buttonholing people, trying to tell them what things were like in the early days. Heck, he was just an ancient town character named Daniel Freeman, "a cantankerous old bird." But look over yonder. There's a pretty ankle.

FREEMAN'S THE NAME

A brass band bragged the mayor to the platform
As the town boys whooped at calico girls
And a bull contemplated a red-eyed cow.
They whistled and cheered at the mayor's oratory,
At his scarecrow stovepipe and politic smile.
Then an auctioneer waved his hat to the crowd:
"None of you can't pass up stock like this!
I know I hear a bid, I hear a bid
On this sorrel mare, this yearling, this heifer,
This here fine upstanding Missouri mule!"
Slowly he wheedled them closer, his stuttered chant
A magic monotone of rhythmic halts.
Some marked the air with calloused fingers.
A few just shuffled off toward the midway
To dare Fatima's tent or the chance of a queen.

A stiff old man, black-frocked and bearded, spat
Dryly into the dust near the entrance booth.
Nearby three smirking fair hands guzzled cider.
One slapped a keg and guffawed, "Look't Mose."
He tilted his jug and even louder said,
"Mose there scalped a goat and stole its beard!"
He passed the jug and slapped the keg again.
"He would of stole the horns, but he's too old."
Like a willow in a storm, the old man straightened.
Cussing, he suddenly swung his cane. One laugher
Ducked behind a keg; one tripped and sprawled;
One clutched his head and dropped the cider jug.

His beard weaving like a flame, old "Mose" stomped off.
Behind him: "That damned old man most broke my head!
That crazy coot! Who in hell was he?"
But Dan'l only muttered to himself,
"Freeman's the name, and by God we mean to cross."

[50]

On the thirtieth of December, 1908, shortly after dark, Daniel Freeman took out his "first death homestead." He was eighty-two years old and had been ailing for more than a year. The GAR conducted the funeral. One of Daniel's lawyers, General L. W. Colby, who had more than once cantered out to the Freeman place on one of his white Arabians, delivered the funeral elegy.

ELEGY

When he let loose the ghost they almost forgot
His rantings against even the holy word,
Sowing sin for Satan in a rainless land.
But since his were not the common blasphemies,
Despite the echoes of his storied rumblings,
At last they took the madman to their hearts.
For though his myth grew bolder, his beard, longer
And more arrogant, as each winter tuned their bones,
The wild old man of tirades turned to friend,
Part of their story and the story of their land.

Dead, he nagged them still, a grump in the wind
Saying, "Move me proper, move me now.
Damnation, I'll unroof the barn," till Frank,
To whom he'd told the spot, returned and pushed them
To dig him up, four heavy-footed sons
Hoisting his bones toward a Nebraska noon,
Four old men laboring beneath his intractable will,
Sure he still would cuss, would damn them for weaklings
If they spilled their father out into the light.
They shouldered his casket in the middle of a field
And marched him northeast to the top of the knoll.
Below him Cub Creek wrinkled like a line across
A palm. And through the glittering layers of wind
He might look toward the always present invisible mountains.

THEY BURIED HIM ON A WIND-SWEPT AFTERNOON

They buried him on a wind-swept afternoon,
Expecting the earth to shudder him down, shake
His bones deep   deep   under the sod.   But no
Stones stirred; except for the wind, no grass tremored,
        Over his grave. Nor could they blot him out.
        His image plowed the landscape of their dreams.

VI

THE LEGACY

In silence they built him the first windowless dwelling in their new land.

Report of the first death of a settler in Gage County, Nebraska (M. W. Ross, winter of 1857)

Early in 1948, a team from the Smithsonian Institution led by J. J. Bauxar began excavations on the site of the Freeman homestead. Between April 5 and May 26, Bauxar and his men established the position of the Freeman buildings. They located the brickyard and kiln and, having checked the stories of "reliable informants," tried to map out the homestead. As a sort of bonus, they even discovered an Indian camp site on high land to the northeast of the Freeman cabin site.

The Smithsonian team worked on land purchased from the Freeman heirs after Congress, on March 23, 1936, had passed an act for the establishment of the Homestead National Monument of America. Congress had directed that the monument should be "a proper memorial emblematical of the hardships and the pioneer life, through which the early settlers passed, in the settlement, cultivation, and civilization of the great West."

THE PURPOSE OF FRAGMENTS

Late April, three years after a war,
The smell of seeded earth
Opens all to life. A bright buzz
Of expectancy flits in the furrows.
Who are these men
Squatting like children at marbles?
At sowing time, they harvest,
Gently crumble the clods, dig up
Not spuds or turnips
But what never sprouted, what happened
At times haphazardly as weeds.
Some day a few mildly curious
May read their log to learn
The tangible way, how they sifted dirt
For certain fragments and found
These scattered pieces of the past:
One harness trapping and a silver spoon;
A jug, somehow still whole,
Near a jagged school slate and
The button of a shoe. What can we know
From such remains
Except the human generalities
Bare of the myth and memory
Whose cloudy substance lingers
Round our lives?
The door of a cast iron range tells us
They cooked, something of their technology.
The fire trench says they knew
What danger was. The silver buttons,
That even pioneers were decorous.
But put Agnes at that stove,

The buttons on Dan'l's jacket,
Notes on the school slate and
Smoke in the air from somewhere
Across Cub Creek, let the mind
Feather the bird
And it will fly.

LEVELS

From out of the arroyo
The Sandia hunters' lances
Pierce the present: giant
Bisons stagger and we walk on thunder.

But those fluted spear heads bedded in bone
Point upward toward a hoe
Or a cord-marked pot
Of water only briefly sipped
In a maize field going quick to sod.
We stamp on all,
Stamp on the prairie grasses
That beckoned the buffalo herds
To shatter fields, crack cobs
And sluiceways under their hooves,
Until the fenceless farmers gave up maize
For meat, back to the ancient way.

On the sites of kerneled dreams
We drop our sandwich wrappers, picnic
On what men rarely can remember
And so call history.

Schooners and Conestogas pitched
Over the backs of buffalo.
Ash ties ribbed the continent anew,
Pinning the tireless hunters to their crumbled loss.

The mixer turns time like cement
As we lower the blocks, level the soddy's
Walls, cut to fireside lengths
The homestead timbers.

[59]

And though after flash floods
Moisture seeps through strata,
What grows is tentative
As a grave or a flower left
To memory or these sifting levels
Underneath a poem.

1826	Born on April 26 in Preble County, Ohio.
1835	Moved to Abington, Knox County, Illinois.
1847	Started to study medicine in Peoria, Illinois.
1849	Supposedly graduated from the Eclectic Medical Institute, Cincinnati, and began to practice in Ottawa, Illinois.
1853	Married Elizabeth Wilbur (three children).
1861	Supposedly enlisted in 17th Illinois Infantry.
1862	Purchased squatter's rights to homestead near Beatrice, Nebraska.
1863	On January 1, shortly after the new year came in, filed for the homestead.
1864	Probably in an engagement with Cheyennes.
1864–1865	Established residence on the homestead.
1865	On February 8 married Agnes Suiter (eight children).
1867–1869	Sheriff of Gage County.
1871	Pre-empted "Court House Square."
1875	Built Freeman School.
1876	Dan and Agnes build the brick house.
1878	Involved in "town lot scandal."
1879	State Supreme Court renders favorable decision in "Court House Square" case.
1886	Sent cane from the homestead to Galusha Grow.
1891	President of The Old Settlers of Gage County.
1892	Attended Independent convention.
1899	Sued school board for turning school into "a place of public worship."
1902	State Supreme Court rules in Freeman's favor.
1903	Supreme Court decision qualified so Bible may be used for literary study in public schools.
	Attended homecoming of Galusha Grow.
1907	Met William Jennings Bryan.
1908	Died on December 30 at 6 P.M.
1909	Funeral on January 2, conducted by GAR.

APPENDIX

DAN FREEMAN'S CLAIM TO BE NUMBER ONE (See page 14)

I have referred to the conflicting stories about how Dan Freeman happened to be in Nebraska at the time he filed his homestead claim and mentioned that Sam Freeman believed his father was a Pinkerton. Sam proudly explained that as a young man Dan Freeman had tracked down a neighbor's stolen horse, and his recovery of the horse caused such a stir that the Pinkertons offered him a job. Sam said that during the rebellion his father, as a Pinkerton, assisted General Price in southern Missouri and took part in the search for Quantrill.

When Freeman was seventy-six years old, his lawyer, W. H. Ashby, gave out another story. Writing in defense of Freeman's claim to be the first homesteader, Ashby recounted Freeman's war experiences in the Omaha *Sunday World Herald,* August 31, 1902. His story sounds even more hyperbolic than Sam's. Freeman, he said, "went in search of information into nearly every state of the Confederacy and carefully examined and reported upon the defenses of the city of Richmond. In Missouri he led an expedition that defeated a guerrilla force in which Colonel Dick Chiles was wounded and taken prisoner, and in which he captured the horses of Senator Stephen B. Elkins' company, and came near capturing the senator himself when he was a simple Missouri bushwhacker."

Dan Freeman's tracks melted in the snows of those early winters. If he did volunteer in Company H of the 17th Illinois Infantry, as the inscription on the monument in front of the Beatrice City Hall says, the records of the Illinois State Historical Library fail to show it. Still, his contemporaries accepted him as a Union veteran. In his day both the *Beatrice Courier* and the *Beatrice Express* referred to him as "an old soldier."

For years, Dan Freeman, and the local newspapers maintained that "his entry was No. 1, his proof of residence was No. 1, his patent was No. 1, recorded on page 1 of book 1 of the land office of the United States" (*Congressional Record—House*, Vol. XXIX, p. 1999). Congressman Galusha Grow, "father of the Homestead Act," used those very words when addressing the House of Representatives on February 19, 1897.

Congress has, in a way, recognized Freeman's claim. The act establishing the Homestead National Monument on the site of the Freeman claim identifies it as the "first homestead entered upon the General Homestead Act of May 20, 1862 . . . ." For historians, however, such recognition does not equal proof. Department of Interior historians tell us that each land office kept its own records, that many land offices issued many applications numbered *1*, and that many final certificates and patents were issued earlier than Freeman's. No single homestead book listing settlers throughout the country existed in Washington. Even so, we are aware of no one who might possibly have filed earlier than Dan Freeman who managed to complete all the requirements and secure the land. He alone of the earliest applicants lived all his life on the land he had thus acquired, and passed it on.

Dan Freeman served as Gage County coroner from after the Civil War until 1871. In 1867, he became bailiff of the Gage County district court, and was elected sheriff two years later. Many old settlers complained that although Freeman could recover stolen property if they kept after him to do so, he could never catch thieves. And so in 1869 L. Y. Coffin got the party nomination for sheriff and Freeman found himself seeking re-election as an independent. The *Beatrice Express* addressed him in print, saying, "Daniel, you have had the office long enough. There are yearnings for a change, and we fear that you must give way." Coffin buried him, 451 to 51.

Even so Daniel continued to hold public office. He served as Justice of the Peace of the Blakely District and as county commissioner (c. 1875). But his reputation for scrupulousness continued to be marred by accusations. After a white man had stolen some ponies from the nearby Oto reservation, the Indian Agent, Major A. L. Green, swore out a warrant for his arrest. The defendant's attorneys, A. Hazlett, and L. W. Colby, had the case tried before Freeman. Their tactics paid off. Although the defendant could produce no bill of sale for the ponies bearing Indian brands, "liberal minded Judge Freeman discharged the defendant and dismissed the case" (*History of Freeman and the First Homestead* by Russell A. Gibbs). Colby and Hazlett each took an Indian pony for fee, but they didn't keep the ponies long. Major Green advised the Indians to lie low near the lawyers' houses and steal the animals back. They did.

Sometimes irate creditors sued Freeman. In June, 1866, Washburn and Company nailed him for $494.33. But Freeman pranced through the courts like a schoolboy through a pasture. It was a game, and the winnings went to the bold.

Dan'l was audacious. Three times he appealed cases to the Nebraska Supreme Court. Twice he won, both times without regard for public sentiment. Who else would pre-empt Beatrice's Court House Square? In 1871 Dan built a small house on the land the town fathers had set aside for a courthouse. He and his family temporarily left the homestead and moved into town. All Beatrice was indignant. So, in 1874 during the absence of the Freeman family the deputy county treasurer, Michael Lynch, seized the opportunity to take back the square for delinquent taxes on other Freeman real estate. At the same time Lynch moved the house Freeman had built into the street and sold it. And just to make sure of keeping Freeman out, the County erected a fence around the block. Dan Freeman sued, but the jury comprised of Beatrice citizens clearly thought the land belonged to Gage County. Freeman had been trying to pull a fast one. The *Express* reported sardonically on March 11, 1875 that someone had asked Dan Freeman "if he intended to hold the fence that the county had built in the court house block." Freeman had a ready answer—he thought "the posts were set deep enough to hold it." But the quipping didn't mean Dan was through. He appealed the case to the Nebraska Supreme Court.

During the summer of 1878 Daniel's claim to the square somehow got mixed up in a plot of certain influential Beatrice citizens, abetted by Mayor Hale, to steal a considerable amount of property. Hale issued a number of false deeds, including one to Daniel Freeman for Court House Square. A mob demanded Hale's resignation, and he wrote it out on the spot. But there were still the deeds. A notification to be served on the recipients of Hale's generosity was drafted at an open meeting. It read: "You are requested to produce before 3 o'clock this afternoon all deeds executed by Hale and all blank deeds in your possession, and all deeds the conveyance of which have been made during Hale's mayorship. . . ." Everyone involved except Freeman gave up their claims to the disputed property. According to the *Gage County Democrat* of August 26, "Freeman is the only obstinate one and it remains to be seen what inducements can be held out to make him disgorge." No inducements were sufficient.

It soon became clear why. In January, 1879, the Supreme

Court repudiated Treasurer Lynch, called him a "trespasser." Despite the town's intention to build a county courthouse on the land Freeman had pre-empted, the land remained Freeman's to sell for his own profit. No one, it seemed, had conveyed title of the land properly to the county.

Dan had remained politically active even after his defeat for sheriff. He had always been helped by his status as the first home-steader—an honor that rubbed off on the town. In August, 1872, he had been elected the Beatrice representative to the state temperance convention, and in that same year the Grand Lodge of I.O.G.T. (International Order of Good Templers) sent him to Lincoln as its representative. Twice in 1874 the *Express* commended him for plans to build first-class houses to rent—he was the kind of man the town was looking for, the paper said. In 1875 he was a member of the Beatrice delegation to Lincoln during Senatorial Week.

But after the "town-lot scandal" and after the Supreme Court had decided the courthouse-square case in his favor, Dan's political influence diminished. Not until 1891 did he re-emerge as a public figure. In that year he was president of the Old Settlers of Gage County. At the state convention of the Independent party he was introduced by a newspaper editor, after which General C. H. Van Wyck, formerly U. S. Senator from Nebraska, proposed three cheers for the first homesteader. Encouraged by this demonstration, Dan tried the next year to win the Independent nomination for state senator. He lost badly. At the convention he tried his old tactics, presenting a gavel made of first homestead timber to the chairman. But he was outclassed by a lady who offered instead a gavel made from the wood of a tree planted at Mount Vernon by George Washington. Even so, Dan wasn't fazed. The *Beatrice Times* of September 13, 1892, describes Freeman as refusing to be the cat's paw for candidates he did not approve, and vigorously "crunching a fresh chew of tobacco between his teeth."

DAN FREEMAN AND THE BIBLE CASE (see page 35)

The members of the school board that Dan Freeman sued were John Scheve, Henry D. Odell, and Matilda Collett, the former one of his close neighbors.

Following Dan's suit, Judge Charles B. Letton issued an alternative writ of mandamus on November 9, 1899. It instructed the school board either to discontinue the activities of which Freeman complained or to appear before the district court and show cause for refusing to do so. The board decided to appear at the appointed time—December 4, at 1:00 p.m. In essence the answer filed by the board admitted Freeman's accusations, but pointedly noted that Dan Freeman was not a member of any church and was an unbeliever. The board defended the teacher, Miss Beecher, maintaining that the ten-minute exercises she conducted "were for the best interests of the pupils." It denied that the exercises were sectarian or dogmatical, noting particularly that the teacher did not comment on the portions of the Bible she read or "force upon . . . any children . . . any of her own notions of church, sectarian, or creed doctrines, faith or beliefs." The board hinted that if anyone was guilty of anything, it was Freeman. He had regularly interfered in school affairs, they complained, and because of him "many of the most efficient school teachers in Gage County will not teach in the district, preferring not to be molested, harassed and hounded."

The controversy was reported by the *Express* from the beginning. A week after the alternative writ had been issued, it called attention to the December 4 hearing in a summary article headlined "Ferninst the Bible." In the same issue (November 16) , the *Express* editorialized, "A respect for the Bible and reverence for the Creator are quite as essential to the true education as equations, dead languages, logic and rhetoric, and the system of education that ignores the former falls far short in the fulfillments of its mission . . . . atheists and sceptics . . . have thus far made little headway. The Bible is safely intrenched in the public schools."

Judge Letton quickly denied Freeman's writ in all particulars. He ruled that such matters were to be determined by the school board. But Freeman was not about to give up. He instructed his attorneys, Franklin J. Griffen and Richard S. Horton, to appeal to the Nebraska Supreme Court.

Not until almost two years later, on October 9, 1902, did the Supreme Court decide that Miss Beecher had violated Article 8, Section 11, of the Nebraska Constitution, which provides that "No sectarian instruction shall be allowed in any school or institution supported in whole or in part by the public funds set apart for educational purposes."

Miss Beecher's testimony undermined the defense. The school board had maintained that Bible reading did not amount to sectarian instruction or an act of public worship. But when Miss Beecher was asked if she read the Bible as a religious exercise, she admitted that her reading was important for that reason. She equated her reading with the offering of prayer; both were part of an act of worship which she thought necessary for herself and her students.

In his opinion, John H. Ames, Supreme Court Commissioner, discussed more than the question of whether Miss Beecher had violated the constitution. His opinion also said that Bible reading, even without commentary, together with the offering of prayers constituted sectarian instruction. To compel a tax payer to support a school in which such exercises were undertaken, Ames indicated, was a violation of the provision that "no person should be compelled to attend, erect or support any place of worship against his consent." Ames stated further: "For more than three centuries it has been the boast and exultation of the Protestants, and a complaint and grievance of the Roman Catholics, that the various translations of the Bible, especially of the New Testament, into the vernacular of different peoples, has been the chief controversial weapon of the former and the principal cause of the undoing of the latter. . . . Books containing such translations have been committed to the flames as heretical and thus translators, printers, publishers, and distributors persecuted, imprisoned, tortured, and put to death. . . ." In Ames' view, therefore, such matters of sectarian difference "are excluded by the express words of the constitution from being taught or in any degree countenanced in educational institutions maintained to any extent by the public funds."

Despite the Supreme Court decision, controversy engulfed the state. Some thought there was a plot, that Freeman was in league with the Catholics. Hadn't Wilbur F. Bryant and John H. Lindale, as friends of the court, introduced arguments in support of Freeman? And Lindale had protested in the name of the Catholic Church. E. O. Kretsinger, attorney for the school board, had asked: "Is it possible that in our schools and universities Plato, Kant, and Felix Adler will be welcome guests, while Jesus of Nazareth is an outlaw?" But the Supreme Court wouldn't listen.

Here and there a few voices reminded enraged citizens that Jews and agnostics did not accept the New Testament as the revealed word of God, that others than Catholics objected to school Bible reading. The *Omaha Daily Bee* and the *Beatrice Express* even ran editorials which seemed to defend the court's decision. But the controversy would not be stilled.

On January 21, 1903, ostensibly for the purpose of denying a rehearing of the case, Chief Justice Sullivan delivered an explanatory ruling. The press responded enthusiastically to this ruling which modified the Ames decision but still awarded Dan Freeman a writ of mandamus. Judge Sullivan reaffirmed that Miss Beecher had violated the constitution although "actuated by the purest and best motives." He elaborated on the Ames decision in order to clarify the status of the Bible in the schools. He recognized that repeated readings of carefully selected passages of the Bible, even without commentary, could well constitute sectarian instruction." But, he pointed out, "Certainly the Iliad may be read in schools without inculcating a belief in the Olympic divinities and the Koran may be read without teaching the Moslem faith. Why may not the Bible be read without indoctrinating children in the creed or dogma of any sect?" The fact that the Bible could be used to inculcate sectarian doctrines "affords no presumption that it will be so used." The Bible, then, might be introduced into schools, but not for sectarian religious purposes. "Alleged violations," Sullivan said, "must be established by competent proof." In the Freeman case such proof had been provided. As for other cases, "The point where the courts may rightfully interfere to prevent the use of the Bible in a public school is where legitimate use has degenerated into abuse."

The Freeman case forced an important and subtle clarification. The decision rendered by the Supreme Court reaffirmed religious freedom in Nebraska without denying the literary magnificence of the Bible or emasculating the public school curriculum.

A NOTE ON SOURCES

This book would have been impossible without the newspaper collection at the Nebraska State Historical Society. I found it necessary to evaluate and to relate contradictory, various, and widely dispersed pieces in the following papers: *Beatrice Daily Express, Beatrice Evening Times, Beatrice Republican, Beatrice Daily Times, Beatrice Courier, Beatrice Daily Sun, Lincoln Star, Lincoln Evening News, Omaha Daily Bee, Gage County Republican, Gage County Democrat,* and *Omaha World Herald.*

Hugh J. Dobbs' *History of Gage County* and *A History of the State of Nebraska* by Alfred T. Andreas provided important leads. The *Portrait and Biographical Album of Gage County, Nebraska* (Chapman Bros.) was also invaluable.

The unpublished manuscript *History of Freeman and the First Homestead* by Russell A. Gibbs in the files of the Homestead National Monument as well as the collection of written and taped interviews there provided important information.

I had occasion, too, to depend on the *Nebraska Farmer,* the *Congressional Record, Nebraska History,* and *Twentieth Century Farmer.* Two articles in particular helped to provide perspective on Dan Freeman's claim to be Number One: "The First Homestead" by Charles Plante and Ray H. Mattison (*Agricultural History,* Vol. 36, No. 4) and "Homestead National Monument: It's Establishment and Administration" by Ray H. Mattison (*Nebraska History,* Vol. 43, No. 1) .

J. J. Bauxar's *Report of Excavations at the Daniel Freeman Homestead* and his daily log notes (National Park Service reports) were enormously helpful. Nor could I have managed without the background material provided in *The Sod House Frontier* by Everett Dick, *The Public Domain* by Thomas Corwin Donaldson, *Pioneer Tales of the Oregon Trail and of Jefferson County* by Charles Dawson, and in numerous works of A. E. Sheldon including *Nebraska Old and New.*

It was exciting to find the trail running by the Freeman Homestead on the "New Map of the Principal Routes to the

Gold Region of Colorado Territory," drawn by August F. Harvey in 1862.

Needless to say, without *Nebraska Reports, Nebraska Supreme Court Reports, Northwestern Reporter,* and *Lawyers Reports Annotated* I would have been unable to deal with Freeman's court experiences.

THE POET

At present, an assistant professor of English at the University of Missouri at Kansas City, Dan Jaffe was born in New Jersey and holds degrees from Rutgers (B.A., 1954) and the University of Michigan (M.A., 1958). His poetry has been widely published, and he is the author of a play, *Some Ticket Holder Wants Your Seat*, produced at the U.M.K.C. Experimental Theater in 1964. Since then he has written the libretto for a jazz opera dedicated to Charlie (Bird) Parker, *Without Memorial Banners*, with a score by Herb Six. First produced in 1966, it has attracted much favorable comment.

THE ILLUSTRATOR

A painter and farmer, Aaron G. Pyle was born in Kansas and now lives at Chappell, Nebraska. He has studied under Thomas Hart Benton, as well as at the Cornish Art School in Seattle and at the Denver Art Institute, and his work has been exhibited in New York and a number of Nebraska cities.